A DANGEROUS PLACE

# A DANGEROUS

 SARABANDE BOOKS, *Louisville, KY*

# PLACE

## CHELSEA B. DESAUTELS

Publisher's Cataloging-In-Publication Data
(Prepared by The Donohue Group, Inc.)

Names: DesAutels, Chelsea B., author.
Title: A dangerous place / Chelsea B. DesAutels.
Description: Louisville, KY : Sarabande Books, 2021
Identifiers: ISBN 9781946448866 (paperback) | ISBN 9781946448873 (e-book)
Subjects: LCSH: Cancer—Poetry. | Pregnant women—Poetry. | Landscapes—Poetry.
American bison—Poetry. | American poetry. | LCGFT: Poetry.
Classification: LCC PS3604.E7572 D36 2021 (print) | LCC PS3604.E7572 (e-book)
DDC 811/.6—dc23

Cover and interior design by Alban Fischer.
Cover art by Xavi Bou.
Printed in Canada.
This book is printed on acid-free paper.
Sarabande Books is a nonprofit literary organization.

   [clmp]

This project is supported in part by an award from the National Endowment for the Arts.
The Kentucky Arts Council, the state arts agency, supports Sarabande Books with
state tax dollars and federal funding from the National Endowment for the Arts.

*For June*

# CONTENTS

III.

*Metastasis* derives from the Greek prefix *meta*, which was used to "express notions of sharing, action in common, pursuit, quest, and, above all, change (of place, order, condition, or nature)." The noun *stasis* is a "stagnation" or "state of motionless or unchanging equilibrium."

I.

# A DANGEROUS PLACE

It seems a beautiful spring though I spend most of it indoors

watching through warped glass small tree buds burst into full green,

the ice crystals on the edge of Lake Nokomis relaxing & spreading

into waves lapping the bottom of bright canoes & sometimes,

near the shore, for the first time this year, a large white heron

landing on spidery legs. An omen, I tell myself: a bird too smart to make

a dangerous place its home & I carry that with me to the hospital.

And I think of the heron when the doctors say congratulations

you're pregnant, let's shine a light to greet your baby.

And I think of the heron when they say oh sorry it seems your womb

is more cavern than nest & no, it's no baby at all.

What have you been feeding this thing. And I think of the heron

skimming the lake surface with spread wings—how could I not—

as we watch on-screen the monster burst into ten thousand gray moths.

And I hear the echo of wings in my belly. And I feel the fury

of wings in my lungs. And when the doctors tuck a port

above my breast I think of the heron disguising a large bed

in marshy grasses. And I imagine the white sheets as heron wings.

And the whirring machines are white eggs.

And the worried voices are sunlight on water.

# SONG OF THE HOUSE BY THE LAKE

in the north I burned cedar: smoked out the ghosts: wrung my neck with baby
teeth & rope: in the north summer leaves turned early: yellow & oak red: my
breasts swelled like gathering thunderheads: I scraped windowpanes: kicked
on the heat: ice fishermen drilled holes to what swam beneath: in the north my
breasts swelled like snake bellies: midwives said use cabbage leaves: in the north
I went looking for mouths found weeds instead: doctors forked my knees took
a shovel & dug: in the north I buried two birds wrapped in a rug: in the north I
couldn't hold what I birthed: I tore down backyard retaining walls ate unearthed
beetles: fake owls kept watch: canoes went unused: in the north something
uninvited grew: I prayed to plastic bags: seeds sprouted heads: in the north my
body rearranged itself: I pulled deer ticks from the back of a thigh: swallowed
soil & gravel no one asked why: in the north there was no time to wean no time
to explain: my grief the neighbor's broken weathervane: in the north smoke rose
from an empty fireplace: out the window winter blue: in the north I willed my
breasts to withered stone fruit

# WHY I THINK OF JUNGLE CROWS

A juniper shrine is lit by ten thousand candles.
One by one, jungle crows carry the candles away

to the fields. The flight does not extinguish
the flame—the wick remains hot. Then, the crows bury

their new light under dry leaves, saving the tallow
in the wax for another day. They'll eat later.

In the hospital, midwives search my womb
for a baby, but there's no heartbeat and no sign

of miscarriage. Still, blood tests show something
somewhere in my body is pregnant. I lullaby

*baby where are you*. The women are getting nervous.
The worshippers can't find their candles. The fields are on fire.

# MYTHOLOGY

At first it was easy to tell the story
because it was actually happening
right then so we could tell each other
the story of how a disease infiltrates
a body but even then we did not recount
all the parts only the best ones
ending with how strong we were
and graceful but it started to get harder
because you had to go back to work
and I was still sick so now it was just me
and new people and most people
don't want to hear your story
of grief unless they knew you before
see grief in a new person is ugly but
I kept practicing because I was hopeful
that one day I might tell the part
about that morning in bed—you remember—
the lake was choppy and it was hot
and raining so we closed up the house—
remember it was you and me
and the baby in bed—she was hungry
and I had to roll away and then we were crying
because we knew it was beyond the point
whether we were strong or graceful
and you were crying too and in fact
I'm still trying to tell that story
or at least write it down but I end up
talking instead about food and baby formula
and freezers of breast milk from strangers
and how to arrange the bags precisely

so the milk doesn't sour and of course
I always mention gratitude because
people like that ending.

# BROKEN PORTRAIT

In Kansas, I hold the baby to my chest in the hallway of a crappy motel. The tornado sirens are loud or soft depending on the wind.

*It's been a long winter, but I'm beginning to brighten,* says my mom, *and we've emptied one of our three storage units.*

The doctors can't decide whether my lungs are blooming with tumors or infection. The weeds look beautiful in the scan, unfolding and growing like psychedelic flowers.

He fills our bathtub hot. Snow falls in the early Minneapolis winter. We watch the water spill over my heaving belly.

No one tells me they've sewn my hymen to the outside of my body. For many reasons, I am afraid of nearness.

*I'm goin' honky-tonkin', get tight as I can, maybe by then you'll 'preciate a good man*—George Jones croons through car speakers.

During cancer I pray to an unfamiliar God. I'm the happiest I've ever been.

When we look up, hundreds of grackle claws on electric wires over the pet food store. In every other direction: no birds.

Once a week, a woman puts gloved fingers inside me. We are trying to reset my brain with clinical experiences.

The neighbor whose name I don't remember draws a chalk outline around my daughter on our porch. It does not wash away, a near-human shape, white on red.

I married a good man. He loves me and irons his own shirts. I'm spoiled.

I mean I am rotting.

# SYMPTOMATIC

Even after stitches
I bled through

cotton & time—

red afternoons,
crimson midnights.

Still they hush women
who complain & anyway

I was busy tending the baby

so I washed my underwear
into rags.

What would you have done?

A woman knows when to bite

her tongue, how to grind
the muscle until there's nothing

but sweet familiar red.

# WHEN TREATMENT ISN'T ENOUGH

The September afternoon is bright green & the fires
        that so often ravage these parts are damped & gone,
leaving only rolling, undulating hills washed in yellow greens
        & blue greens & occasionally, over the second ridge,
a solitary oak tree, bark chipped from buffalo hides.

I left my family to come here because I'm trying to
        stay alive. I shift the car into neutral & roll quietly,
unobtrusively, toward the herd, which ripples & swells
        like little bluestem in the breeze, a cool breeze
that comes down from the north where it is already winter

& offers a whiff of the coming season to the buffalo who,
        I suppose, take note as it grazes their coats.
They don't mind me settling in here, rolling down the windows
        to watch unobstructed their yearling calves romp & roll
in soft dirt, the cow buffalo grazing & keeping watch of the babies,

the bulls off somewhere else, perhaps by the stream
        under the oak tree & now one young male throws
his head & grunts, ambles toward the car & proceeds to scratch
        his shoulder on the hood, showing off his courage.
I unwrap the scarf from my head & let the breeze wash over

my scalp. These beasts have offered me sanctuary
        so many times, I sometimes feel as though I speak
with them, as if I see my own reflection in the black pools
        of their eyes, as if, when they look up from the grass
& catch my gaze, they are saying to me, welcome,

you're home now, you're one of us.

      I have felt this my whole life, this generosity,
these well wishes from the wild herd.

      I'm not here for new prayers;
only to rest among the old.

# BURIAL

When Mom dies, she wants her body
thrown on a slash pile.

Grandpa makes the best ones, but he won't
be around, so I'll do what he taught me:

gather lumber on needled ground,
branches felled by lightning

& old nurse logs no longer
useful to younger trees.

Build a pyramid, then wait—
you can't burn until a true freeze hits

or flames will vault their boundaries.
Understand, we haven't had a good

forest fire here for years.
We burn brush to protect ourselves.

On the drive home last night,
small fires glowed on the side of a mountain—

amber pockets against the snow.
You have to hold someone very close

to undress her to her bones, to carry
her naked body to a hillside & strike a match.

# SONG OF THE BLACK HILLS

in the hills I began to grow hips: to push outward with bones & with flesh: I found old bottles & torn scarves by the creek bed: in the hills I misunderstood my indignation where it came from: I wore red hair down my back: I lived alongside one woman's descent into a bathroom puddle never asking why the floor was wet: at the cabin bats flew overhead: in the hills I climbed up the notch down devil's bathtub: I found owl pellets & knew then what they were: I held mouse skulls & felt my own bones unwind: I stopped wearing a brace to straighten my spine never trusted the men who said I'd grow bent: in the hills I kissed boys over canyons: I sought out: called out to the sky: in the hills I did not apologize did not perceive a mother might turn away: I saw a buffalo give birth in grass learned the placenta comes last: I took my brother & sister & hid under the desk: in the hills I was sacrificed but not like I thought: in the hills pines grew from rock: roots caught rainwater in cracks: in the hills animals rise after birthing & eat what's left

# SURGERY IS CONTRAINDICATED

My daughter ate my wedding ring.

We've watched & waited & worried, but there's been no sign
of the ring, now surely snuggled up forever inside an intestine.

And so what? Find me one person who hasn't swallowed the past
& lost it inside the body. Of course, doctors explained the steps required

for expulsion: the anesthesia, the cutting & the costs. But even when you know
the shape of the thing, you can't always predict its course.

~~~~~

Once, in pain, I begged to be sliced open, expecting a smooth removal,
a few well-placed sutures, a bottle of pills,

maybe, some flowers by the bed, but when the skin was splayed
we found the copper memory I'd swallowed had dissolved

or shape-shifted, my body more conductive than before, my tongue
more metallic & where I used to be hollow,

a jangling.

~~~~~

Doctors say excavation is more dangerous than living
with a rock in your gut.

Maybe it's the unavoidable confrontation with your personal geology:

what conspired to form those fossils,
what absorbed those living things.

How you ate them. How they became you.

I've heard eating crystals can offer protection. I don't know if that's true.
But when I watch my daughter gather quartz & mica

& river rock, building small mountains with care,
I swear she's in a state of meditation or grace.

Who am I to judge how she fingers those stones, how she opens
her soft mouth, or what she's called to put there?

# INTERNET SUPPORT GROUP

In the shade of a maple tree, on a grassy hill,
        three women laid hands on me.

One saw a cave in my hips. Another felt bricks
        rising from a brook. The last heard a bellow

from deep within the woods. We were strangers
        come together to spend an afternoon

drinking tea & sharing stories of cellular bad luck,
        then suddenly makeshift healers

summoning our mothers' lessons on touch—
        on heat & symmetry, tenderness & release.

From above, we might have looked like sundials
        or spokes on a round knitting loom.

We wanted so badly to believe
        in our ministry we ignored the obvious.

That milk thistle grows here because of stolen land.
        The auspicious arrival of geese is the result of

migratory patterns. Even the static inside our cells
        likely explainable by simple division.

It's embarrassing, sometimes, how far I'll go
        searching for unprecipitated magic,

how much I'll trust that pine air cures cancer

    or the hawk overhead is only keeping watch.

## II.

# THE AMERICANS

When you get home, I won't be wearing

    the wig I bought to hide

my scalp so you'll have nothing to take

    off me. I'll meet you at the door.

I'll want to ask how you know if you love

    someone enough. I'll want to ask

what happens if all this time you mistook

    yourself for a real person. It's raining.

Come home. We'll watch the show

    where the husband and wife perform

love by kissing passionately

    in the kitchen before leaving to spy

for a secret country. It's about what we tell

    each other and what we don't.

You won't say the trip was better without me.

I won't tell you how I slinked

around in a housecoat, carrying a teacup

of dark tequila, and the silence

was a symphony blooming in every corner.

Come home, I miss you.

I've put away the wig, it's too brunette.

It's just me here. I have no secret

country.

# SONG OF THE BAYOU CITY

in Texas rain sank the earth: the city sang its bayous: I learned the weight of humidity wrapping its legs around you: in Texas doctors removed my plastic heart: heat contaminated choice: I paid a professional to activate nerves between my legs: in Texas fear was a rising river a bright depression: all the bats died: I lost all sense of time: in Texas even animal meat wasn't enough: I ate organs & pills & gave away blood: in Texas possums ran for shelter: I packed a bag for the roof: between my legs scar tissue a bayou slicing through industry: I was a ghost with domestic responsibilities: floodwater licked the front steps: marriage got hard: in Texas water from the spout ran dangerous & gold: I followed animals back to their home: held irresponsible anger irrepressible shame: in Texas a stranger asked if I had a community of faith: locked things exploded: I drank oil & gas: pomegranates on the counter rotten & black: in Texas I watched pelicans dive at the beach dropped to my knees that I might be as hungry as their open beaks

# IF IT TURNS OUT PREGNANCY CAUSES CANCER

it's almost too obvious to say the dualities of life can no longer be ignored the
fact that you're not keeping hand-me-downs that you're selling the stroller can
no longer be ignored right now my daughter is tracking dog ears in dotted lines
with a small black pen & asking what do I do next mama what next how do I
make the animal complete what is still missing if I fill the space with black ink
if I color it dark & permanent am I done with this exercise can I put it away love
I say the numbers come to an end you can stop anytime

# LANDSCAPE AT THE CHINATI FOUNDATION

*after Donald Judd's* 15 untitled works in concrete

I select a border, cement bending sunbeams
      around corners—

                                          back home the storm
                                    drove the ground lower
                                    this is not a metaphor

like empty boxcars under a desert sky, here, I choose
      my geography, which grasses & brush to see

                                      I left soon after the flood

here, clouds are swirling & I, too, am shape-shifting

                                        as I traveled south
                              my organs rearranged themselves

in & out of shadow & light; I, too, was anticipated—
      a guest in a field of buffalo grass—

when they found it
they said don't worry
this cancer makes a feast
of a uterus but
probably won't kill you


& I, too, am moved by the scale of the mountains,
by the forces that raised the earth or carved it down


I was familiar already
with delivering my insides
to something unknown


by the chorus of grasshoppers who made this switchgrass home


at night
tumors burst
like supernovas


& the small yellow petals exploding from clay loam—


they said soldier cells
would tidy up the masses
turned to dust


& I measure the sky against these slabs

                                                        now I'm clean


count sagebrush on the axis—Indian grass seedheads
                awash in afternoon—


                                        after this I'll get kebabs
                                from a food truck in a dry art town
                                        & swim in the motel pool


the atmosphere, locals say, ignites at dusk—


                                        I'll draw my arm
                        steady across the water's surface
                                palm open & strong


in the distance, red lights melting


                        & separating


        against the dark

# GHOST CHILD

All day the sun moved over the rock I sat on.
All day I tried to think like an elk.
I'd been drinking bad wine
from a thermos and counting the blades
on little bluestem. It was nearly dark
when they finally appeared under the gnarled oak,
brown legs in prairie grass. And there's the bull—
disappearing into the blackening sky.
Why did I come here, to get drunk among
the glade moss and deer flies? Why not sit
at the kitchen table or in the leather armchair?
Back then they told me I'd never actually been
pregnant (the test a false positive, the blood
unrelated, the swelling in my belly something
else) and my husband's face turned to mine.
What kind of body prefers cancer to a child?
But I did not want that baby.
The bull has already shed his velvet.
In two seasons, his testosterone will plummet
and his antlers will fall off in a late-spring snow.
And he'll go about his life, mating and grazing,
indistinguishable from the females.

# SHEDDING

my father says there's a buck
circling home with velvet antlers

whose eyes during this season
alone pulse red—

it's the hunters' theory why
on the leeward side of lookout

mountain a pair of eyes
might meet you shining like harvest

moons him watching
you & you gazing into blood

pools gleaming red
like that november all the boys hid

in the woods waiting
for something to hang

on their bedroom walls & the girls
glistening in raspberry

lotion walked the mall
wide-eyed & yielding as fawns

# LATE-SEASON OUTDOOR WEDDING

The night before, we'd eaten fried walleye
with tartar sauce in a big white tent and passed
a whiskey-filled quaich to loved ones
who sipped and offered blessings. There was music.
You played guitar. I went to bed early, happy.
You joined me later, happy. The next morning,
we woke to snow and gray skies. All morning long,
I cried and heaved and my mother and bridesmaids
whispered, afraid I was having my doubts. I wasn't.
It was my wanting to be good at loving
and wanting everything, like a river island
suddenly shorn from the bank and flooded by ice melt.
To stay warm, we lit small fires under the arch; we said our vows
in wood smoke. And I thought I'd done it.
I thought I'd sworn all of me to someone else.
As if that's what you wanted.

# MORNING COMMUTE

If the thousands of starlings in the sky
above Houston right now—

diving and swooping in concert, a black fog
darting over the interstate searching for seed

by the bayous and littered intersections—if they know
something we don't, how to read the air,

how to choose a new direction all together like a soft fold
in a silk bathrobe being smoothed away,

should we make something of it?

Every morning, she and I watch them out the car window.
It's a game. We don't bother guessing when the birds will swerve.

The trick is predicting the moment before.

# EVIDENCE

Last night, a strange noise from the road
at high frequencies, like alien bodies of static.
I search for evidence of the skirmish.
Leaves lie torn at the base of a young tree.
Nearby, a small animal's scat. Possums,
maybe, so I pull up videos of possum sounds.
In one, a man uses a blue plastic broom to corner
a scared possum on a concrete floor.
It shrieks & cries & I have to walk away,
the static still ringing in my chest. Like how,
when my anxiety is high, I screech
*You're not loving me right* at the people I love most.
Oh, I'm a mess of greed & expectation
& those are just the ones I've the gall to look at.
Some nights, though, when the sun's almost down,
I sit on the porch & watch this bass jump
above the lake, then dive back into the dark water—
down low with the weeds & hollow reed stems—
& I think of my daughter safely inside,
rolling over in her small bed, maybe drawing
a pale blue blanket a little closer to her cheek
& there goes the bass again & the night is quiet
except for these small interruptions
& I say *thank you*—that's it, just *thank you*—
without asking to whom I think I'm speaking
or whether they're listening.

# WATER COMMUNION

On the sanctuary wall where I'd expect Christ
hangs a wrought-iron bird—large, wings spread—
& I can't find any reason not to believe
it's a heron. Which is to say, yes, I'm still
assigning meaning to wings & yes, you can
make anything mean anything you need.
Take this church: I needed hope
& these tall carved doors opened to a bird.
Or last week: I missed the water communion
so I watched the sermon online.
The congregation brought water
from their summer travels or bathtub
or rain caught in a birdbath in the backyard.
One by one, members emptied water
into a clay pot. A man spoke about water
as mother & water as destroyer
& water as god. Then the video cut out.
But the service wasn't over—the lesson
was unresolved. Like when I was sick, how I'd fall
asleep before the end of guided meditation.

# COVENANT

One morning, all the nuns in the convent
started meowing,

mewing and purring until even the holy roof
above them arched and curled,

a feverish chorus
slinking around the Christ figure's legs.

Then it ended. The nuns
gathered for dinner in silence.

But the meowing had been unbearable
to the townsmen. So they arrived with leather

and horses, and whipped the animal
from each woman. And that's the thing about marriage.

You take a vow. You give up your animal.

# AFTER THE DIAGNOSIS

It was a long time before we had sex again.
First there was the fear. Then the pain
and the fear. We settled into it, I suppose,
my retreat, how I coiled tight my desire
like the root ball I once found
strangling a nugget of fool's gold.
Not even the center of my longing
was authentic. The problem with disease
is that you have to keep asking yourself
what's different now and what's not.
It's a matter of survival: a plant alive
in the wild tends its dark roots underground.
One that's been dug up and brought inside,
though—that kind of plant has its roots teased
and sliced so they'll go reaching
for new soil. What am I afraid of?

III.

# HOT BLOOD

I just finished reading a children's story. I almost didn't want it to end,
the smell of clean, wet toddler hair in my lap, the story about

the elephant who fears his pig friend is making him sneeze, who worries
they can't be friends anymore, only to learn he's suffering from

the common cold, plain & simple. Outside, the Texas rain is flooding
our dark streets again, which is something I'm starting to get used to now

that we've lived here two years, something, I remind myself, which is not
going to kill people every time, only the worst times & that is probably not

tonight. You're taking our child by the hand, leading her to bedtime songs
& one more story, maybe the one we made up that ends

with the bear inviting the wolf to a birthday party in the cave. It's a pretty solid story
though I worry we haven't made the wolf suffer the consequences

of stealing the party flowers quite enough. It's strange to find myself a mother,
in Texas, writing poems about the rain, when I used to spend so much of my time

walking through drifts of snow in dark boots. Now I keep those boots in a box
in the detached garage, hopeful I'll need them again. Remember when the lake

froze & we'd take the dog out on the ice? That was before I got sick.
When you come back to the couch, you tell me a story about the Dancing Plague of 1518

which you think might make good poem fodder. I like the sound of your voice
& besides, my brain has been a little mushy lately, I've been feeling

my feelings too much & not saying the things I mean to when I speak,
so I like the idea of sitting here, quietly, listening to you.


On the other side of the wall, the rain is really coming down but this is not
a tropical depression, so the rivers probably won't overflow their banks


tonight, the city won't sink. Apparently, you begin, one woman started dancing
& couldn't stop & soon the whole town went nuts, jiving & jerking, dancing themselves


to death, fifteen people a day. The government ruled out the suspected cause
after determining the town had not, in fact, been cursed by a saint. Instead,


the government, applying science to fact, deduced the dancers had "hot blood."
Did they prescribe bloodletting, I want to know, imagining a medieval village


on its knees, weeping with gratitude as the dancers finally slow, standing at the riverbank,
blood dripping from each wrist into the quiet current, the one they trust to carry


the disease away, down to the next town. No, you say, get this: the government built a stage
& hired musicians, the cure was simply to dance more. It didn't work & the death toll was high.


You take my hand in yours, which feels sweeter than usual.
Is that the whole story, I ask.

# FOUR YEARS LATER

So this is my life, then. Peppermint oil in the mornings.
A pink ceiling. One low-hanging electrical wire at the bottom
of the basement stairs where a child calls for help
unpacking her costumes, slippery in their brown
paper boxes. For years I was undiagnosable.
Then I wasn't. And you'd think almost dying
would make every minute count. It doesn't.
I mean, sometimes walking down
a shaded block is enough. But sometimes a small voice
swims up the staircase and then I'm suspended
out of time. She says Mama and I'm surprised
to be addressed. Not a ghost but not quite real.
I wait to see who she's calling for.

# SELF-PRESERVATION

I can make an omelet
but I can't convince you
      to keep the eggs

on the counter
like they do in Europe.
      And why not?

In an artisan shop
I buy a hand-shaped
      clay carton glazed

in purple and blue—
twelve gleaming depressions.
      I bring it home

and show you: in each hollow,
we'll rest eggs the freckled ecru
      of our daughter's

early summer skin;
after we crack the eggs,
      we'll slide their insides

into a copper pan
shimmering with full-fat
      Irish butter. The yolks will glow

autumn gold, not yellow
like the ones from the store.
        The farm delivered them.

Look, these are beautiful,
delicate eggs. Look,
        the clay carton is a sign

we're living
a meditative life—
        that our home is full

of slow mornings.
See? Each little egg is safe
        in its prairie-sky-at-twilight

recession. They won't roll
away. We've made them
        too meaningful.

# BLACK HILLS

1.

Fake lightning cracks across the sky of the Passion Play.
I never grow used to the flash of radiance, or the darkness ringing up the canyon after.

For every church, a bar. For every meadow, a failing Kmart.
For every soft breeze through pines, a memory I'm trying to lose.

Under our feet: hundreds of miles of caverns. Wind Cave. Jewel Cave.
An entire world of water dripping slowly in empty rooms.

Hells Angels ride winding blacktop from Custer to Sturgis.
They park their bikes in a straight line downtown, saloons on each side.

At the top of the canyon, we kiss in the backseat, shock of yellow leaves in headlights.
Below us, classmates enter a small cave to drink beer. Everyone here emptying or filling space.

I'm happiest driving grassy foothills at dusk, looking for buffalo.
I like the old bulls best: separated from the herd, scratching their worn hides on tree bark.

2.

The football star runs up Higgins Gulch. Finds a man's skull crushed on a rock.
The high school principal says he knows more than one boy showing anger like that.

Loneliness is unavoidable: winter is barren, summer is dry, spring is crowding.
In autumn I try to exhale, but a school of shimmering minnows swims right past me.

Three times a week, a thunderclap informs the town that Jesus has risen again.
Even the dogs learn to ignore the clatter.

In 1900, two prospectors discover the earth is sighing cold air from a hidden mouth.
They use dynamite to create an entrance large enough for tourists.

How do we love a landscape but not a place?
How to return & still forget?

Symbiosis: small-winged birds eating insects off buffalo backs.
I search my memory for other proof of interdependence.


3.


Downtown Sturgis. A heavy middle-aged woman in tassels & a flowing blonde wig.
A new angel gliding past Harleys in biker boots.

Jewel Cave breathes in & out with atmospheric changes.
We're not to touch the spar crystals, tarnished with the oil of tourist hands.

By the creek, an old fishhook caught in debris. I know he loves me.
I've understood twice when to love someone back. Once it was not too late.

Buffalo my pumping heart. Tongue: rainbow trout in a low-running stream.
Memory an antelope in a crown of wildflowers, thrashing.

Gold draws white men to the Black Hills.
The Great Sioux Reservation shrinks, shrinks again. Shrinks again.

I sleep in the bed under the glass-eyed elk & arrow.
I am learning to pray to no one in particular.

4.

Consider the view from a girl's perspective: a leather-skinned biker with pierced nipples.
Through each ring, a heavy chain. Ahead of her: a man, a beer, the end of the leash.

In the car he wants to know what makes me feel good.
I tell him honestly: I have no idea.

Vendors sell tourists smoothed quartz & tickets to pan for fool's gold.
I find mica in the gravel two-track, peel each layer into translucence.

One memory I pull from the depths: Sitting by French Creek alone.
Shaving my legs in creek water. The razor under stippled current. Blood swimming away.

Homestake Gold Mine closes. I stand at the metal fence over the quarry.
This whole place is just holes & filled holes. What used to be.

All seasons, the freezer is full of animal: elk, deer, turkey, pheasant.
I eat everything my father kills.


5.

Police are slow to solve the Higgins Gulch case. They're unpracticed.
Here, most murders are small ones. Domestic.

The chained woman & her leader enter the Loud American Roadhouse.
She tries to dance to the Garth Brooks cover band, writhing in little jerks.

French Creek my veins. Jewel Cave my mouth.
Needles Highway a mother's outstretched hand, reaching.

Dirt red as my hair stretches toward God.
I hold service in the woods while vultures swarm overhead.

Black Hills gold is pink & green & cast in small rosettes.
We wear it in our ears, around our necks.

Above the quarry, stars move in & out of clouds like memories briefly caught
& released, like trout too small to eat.

# CITY LAKE

Almost dusk. Fishermen packing up their bait,
a small girl singing *there's nothing in here nothing in here*
casting a yellow pole, glancing at her father.
What is it they say about mercy? Five summers ago
this lake took a child's life. Four summers
ago it saved mine, the way the willows stretch
toward the water but never kiss it, how people laugh
as they walk the concrete path or really have it out
with someone they love. One spring the path teemed
with baby frogs, so many flattened, so many jumping.
I didn't know a damn thing then. I thought I was waiting
for something to happen. I stepped carefully
over the dead frogs and around the live ones.
What was I waiting for? Frogs to rain from the sky?
A great love? The little girl spies a perch
just outside her rod's reach. She wants to wade in.
She won't catch the fish and even if she does
it might be full of mercury. Still, I want her
to roll up her jeans and step into the water,
tell her it's mercy, not mud, filling each impression
her feet make. I'm not saying she should
be grateful to be alive. I'm saying mercy
is a big dark lake we're all swimming in.

# WOLF SONG, OR, THE WOMAN UNBOUNDED

in the woods I grow wild: grow wild fur it mats: I catch myself on a branch
pull hard to remove my gnarledness: in the woods pain is not a sign of what has
happened what might come it is a burr in my paw a hunger in my gut: in the
woods I do not hunt resolution: my undercoat is bristled or smooth: each night
my eyesight improves: I walk through tall grasses indivisible from home: in the
woods I am no one: or I am the rotting leaves I spring from: my black nose blends
into a black tree: I do not roam in their backyards I am not lonely: in the woods
I am undomesticated: formless: only a body: in the woods I wander overlapping
territories bald eagles above black bears there are no boundaries: I shake loose
a deer fly: I am childless & strong: in the woods I tread on dried needles & sun-
bleached hip bones: track north by wildflowers I follow the seeds: in the woods I
wail however I need: in the woods I am unbecoming: unmothered: unmothering

# TO MY DAUGHTER IN SPRINGTIME

If you ever catch a mayfly by the kitchen sink
break its legs to pieces feel a little glory in the killing
though it was accidental if you ever eat all the honey
we bought to trap raccoons lick the salt block
on the tree stump pull apart a green branch just to see
what it looks like inside if you ever stick a piece of trash
in a prairie dog hole curious whether the animal can still
breathe down there or watch a trout squirm & kick on the creek
gravel gasping even if you unravel every thread of yarn
in the bird nest I showed you yesterday & even if the little
blue eggs fall through their ruined home toward a concrete
driveway covered in chalk rainbows I want you to know
none of us knows what to do with wonder not one of us
knows how to love the world

# HOME AGAIN

I'm trying to remember what this place
will be like in winter. How much whiskey,
which snow tires to outlast the season.
I've been gone a long time. They say last year
was the most brutal winter yet, but I keep picturing
the winter we fell in love. We were so shy,
despite ourselves, and the snow kept coming
and the city closed down and everything settled
into a white sigh. The snow buried your car
so we tied up our boots and stepped out
my apartment door into the lamplight.
There was no sound save for the cross-country
skiers gliding along Bryant Avenue.
All the shops were closed. We cut the first tracks
down the sidewalk. I knew I'd spend my life with you
before that night, but I didn't know what we'd face,
how many times we'd think the world was safe
and blanketed in stillness, and be wrong.
Tonight, before bed, you're going to pour me
a small glass of whiskey without asking
and I'm going to take it upstairs to drink while I read.
Later this year, it's going to snow and we'll have
to figure out winter all over.

# NEARLY ENOUGH

Black-capped chickadees singing their morning song.

The sun rising over the notch.

How many times have I sat on this bench and watched the sky above the pines
forge from orange to blue?

Past the bend, French Creek pushing dead leaves through a beaver's dam.

# WATCHING MY DAUGHTER SLEEP, I REMEMBER WHEN DOCTORS SAID MY BREAST MILK WOULD BECOME TOXIC

How could you know what it means
        that in winter I softened chicken livers

with shallots and butter, fed you with a spoon?

How I fought to put a piece of myself into everything
        that nourished you.

I would have braided my hair into challah

        for Saturday-morning French toast
        if I'd had any hair left.

Even now, even when we can't afford it, I feed you
        organic blueberries,

sweeten your spinach muffins

with pure maple syrup. Even now

        I buy you cold-pressed
        carrot juice with probiotics

and put it on a credit card. It is not frivolous.

And I'm not telling you this to prove my sacrifices.

I'm as regret-soaked as anyone.
      As you will be.

Loving you is the orchard creek freezing from the bottom up—
      bewildering,


           crowding.

Like lightning to the apple branch,

it splits me.

# MAYBE YOU NEED TO WRITE A POEM ABOUT MERCY

Start this one with the woman standing at the edge
of the woods. Or the desert, it doesn't matter,
what matters is she's standing under a darkening sky
and she knows, at this point, having spent months
in the hospital, that there's nothing she can do—
no threshold between threat and tranquility,
no demarcation she can draw around herself
or her child for protection, everything is actually
everything else, the stone just kicked
and whatever comes next are the same.
And, knowing this, a great emptiness swells
inside her stomach, an airiness she could float away on—
and the night bellows and the sun rings once more
then slips under the horizon. Maybe then:
a humming of an old tune, her own hand
stroking her red hair. Mercy.

As in the story the man on the bus told me
about his late wife, how by the end she'd forgotten
their wedding, even, and their children's names,
and once she went missing in the depths of winter
dead bent on saving the cattle from the blizzard
that years ago left all the calves frozen
on their sides. He told me his wife saw angels.
It was her last day, she was at home and the nurse
called him to the living room where the bed was.
His wife asked, Do you see them? And he said,
Yes. And together they counted the wings.
When he told me this story, the man wasn't sad.
He had just picked up groceries to make bread—

he missed fresh bread, he said, and so
he bought yeast and flour and fine kosher salt.
He wanted to watch the dough rise.

Because the man wasn't sad, I tried not to be sad,
too. He smiled and got off the bus. Out there,
the streetlamps flickered and the cold night grew
and off he went to warm his kitchen. I waved
and wondered if there's a word for the way
joy and pain are the same, how, if we're lucky,
they thread us like an electrical wire cuts a tree,
and there we stand, tender and green, reaching,
charged, humming.

# ANNUAL MIGRATION

After three days of rain, this morning
is streaked as golden as the thin crust
on the baguettes at the bakery
down the road from where I'm walking,
watching the swallows descend
on the cattail tops, which are all rushing a bit
southeast in the wind, the maple
nearby the only one reddening its leaves
this early in the season. The baby is wrapped
to my chest. I've walked as far as I can today.
Overhead, a skein of Canada geese marks
the inevitable decline of temperatures,
a great continental journey. I didn't know
what motherhood would feel like.
One day she just appeared and all the ancient
wooden joints in my heart clicked into place;
the whole thing started thrumming.
And now—you know what, I've changed my mind.
I want to leave the cancer out of this poem.
She's soft as goose feather, fast as a fleet
of sparrows, unpredictable as the flash
of cardinal in the reeds.

# ACKNOWLEDGMENTS

I owe many people thanks. First, to my teachers, Kevin Prufer, Martha Serpas, Jennifer Chang, Nick Flynn, and the late Tony Hoagland—thank you for your patience, gentle shoves forward, and friendships. Poetry is less unfamiliar, and all the more delightful in its mystery, thanks to time spent with you. And to Alden Smith, my eleventh-grade English teacher who recited Robert Frost's "Directive" in the snow, you may have set all this in motion.

Thank you to L. Lámar Wilson and Robin Davidson for your wisdom and encouragement.

I am grateful to the institutions that provided time and opportunity to write: the University of Houston Creative Writing Program, Inprint, the Loft Literary Center, the Anderson Center at Tower View, the Community of Writers, Minnesota Northwoods Writers Conference, Writers in the Schools, Vermont Studio Center, Fine Arts Work Center, and Poetry at Round Top. Thank you to the friends and teachers who fill those spaces.

Much gratitude to friends who read early iterations of this manuscript with care and generosity, among them: Lauren Berry Shellberg, Michelle Burk, Joshua Gottlieb-Miller, Niki Herd, Christopher Brean Murray, Michelle Orsi, Dallas Saylor, Sam Thilén, Cait Weiss Orcutt, and Theodora Ziolkowski.

Thank you to Mayflower Early Childhood Center in Minneapolis, MN, and Montessori Country Day School in Houston, TX, for providing rich and loving environments for June while I studied and wrote.

Thank you to Dr. Peter Argenta at the University of Minnesota Health Cancer Care and Dr. Shannon Westin at the University of Texas MD Anderson Cancer Center. The quality and heart of your care is unmatched. To the oncology nurses in the East Bank Hospital at the University of Minnesota Medical Center, I consider you my angels.

To our friends in the Twin Cities and across the country, who showed up for our family in unimaginable ways, thank you. We are so lucky.

Many thanks to the DesAutels family, who welcomed me with love, good food, and laughter.

To Sarah Gorham, Jeffrey Skinner, and the entire team at Sarabande: the privilege of working with you is boundless, as are the instinct and intellect with which you bring books into the world. Thank you for giving my words a home.

And, finally, to my family, who cared for us during the storm, and always. Mom, Dad, Reilly, Caila, and Britney, thank you for holding June when I couldn't. Thank you for holding me.

John and Pat, I have spent my life in the glow of your unconditional love.

To Zac—your kindness, intelligence, and humor steady me and give me faith. Sharing our lives is one of my great fortunes.

And, of course, to June—my greatest teacher. You, my love, are transformation itself.

⁓⁓⁓

Thank you to the editors of the following journals, in which these poems first appeared, sometimes in earlier versions and under different titles:

*The Adroit Journal*: "Song of the Bayou City"

*Copper Nickel*: "A Dangerous Place" and "Mythology"

*Gigantic Sequins*: "Song of the House by the Lake"

*Grist*: "Surgery Is Contraindicated"

*The Massachusetts Review*: "Ghost Child," "Covenant," "After the Diagnosis," "City Lake," and "Annual Migration"

*The Missouri Review*: "Water Communion" (Poem of the Week), "Watching My Daughter Sleep, I Remember When Doctors Said My Breast Milk Would Become Toxic," and "Maybe You Need to Write a Poem about Mercy"

*New Ohio Review* (online): "Late-Season Outdoor Wedding"

*Ninth Letter*: "Self-Preservation"

*Notre Dame Review*: "Song of the Black Hills"

*Passages North*: "Burial"

*Ploughshares*: "Why I Think of Jungle Crows"

*Redivider*: "Symptomatic"

*Salt Hill*: "The Americans"

*Sixth Finch*: "If It Turns Out Pregnancy Causes Cancer" and "Hot Blood"

*Tupelo Quarterly*: "Broken Portrait"

*Willow Springs*: "Black Hills" and "To My Daughter in Springtime"

Thank you to the editors of the *Missouri Review* for selecting "Watching My Daughter Sleep, I Remember When Doctors Said My Breast Milk Would Become Toxic" and "Maybe You Need to Write a Poem about Mercy" as winners of the 2020 Jeffrey E. Smith Editors' Prize.

# NOTES

The definitions in the epigraph are courtesy of *Oxford English Dictionary Online*'s entries, 2020.

"Song of the House by the Lake," "Song of the Black Hills," "Song of the Bayou City," and "Wolf Song, or, The Woman Unbounded" take inspiration from C. D. Wright's "Song of the Gourd" (*Steal Away: Selected and New Poems*, published by Copper Canyon Press, 2002).

"Why I Think of Jungle Crows" takes inspiration from Peter Harris's "Why I Think of the Young Albatross."

"When Treatment Isn't Enough" takes inspiration from C. K. Williams's "On Learning of a Friend's Illness" (*Tar*, published by Vintage Books, 1983).

"Landscape at the Chinati Foundation" is after Donald Judd's *15 untitled works in concrete* (1980–1984), a large-scale exhibit in Marfa, Texas.

"Hot Blood" takes inspiration from Larry Levis's "God Is Always Seventeen" (*The Darkening Trapeze*, published by Graywolf Press, 2016).

"To My Daughter in Springtime" takes inspiration from Kim Addonizio's "To the Woman Crying Uncontrollably in the Next Stall" (*Nasty Women Poets: An Unapologetic Anthology of Subversive Verse*, published by Lost Horse Press, 2017).

"Maybe You Need to Write a Poem about Mercy" takes inspiration from Robert Hass's "Faint Music" (*Sun Under Wood*, published by Ecco Press, 1996).

# CHELSEA B. DESAUTELS

's work appears in the *Adroit Journal, Copper Nickel, Massachusetts Review, Ninth Letter, Pleiades, Ploughshares,* and elsewhere. Winner of the Jeffrey E. Smith Editors' Prize from the *Missouri Review,* Chelsea earned an MFA from the University of Houston, where she was the recipient of the Inprint Paul Verlaine Prize in Poetry. She also holds degrees from Wellesley College and the University of Minnesota Law School. Chelsea lives with her family in Minneapolis.

SARABANDE BOOKS is a nonprofit literary press located in Louisville, KY. Founded in 1994 to champion poetry, short fiction, and essay, we are committed to creating lasting editions that honor exceptional writing. For more information, please visit sarandebooks.org.